What Is the Story of Ebenezer Scrooge?

by Sheila Keenan

illustrated by Andrew Thomson

Penguin Workshop

For Paula: Merry, merry!—SK

For Cerys and Rhia—AT

PENGUIN WORKSHOP
An imprint of Penguin Random House LLC, New York

First published in the United States of America by Penguin Workshop,
an imprint of Penguin Random House LLC, New York, 2022

Visit us online at penguinrandomhouse.com.

Library of Congress Control Number: 2022021870

Printed in the United States of America

ISBN 9780593226025 (paperback)   10 9 8 7 6 5 4 3 2 1 WOR
ISBN 9780593226032 (library binding)   10 9 8 7 6 5 4 3 2 1 WOR

Contents

What Is the Story of Ebenezer Scrooge?

There is a tidy row of nineteenth-century brick town houses on Doughty Street in London, England. Behind the cheery red door at number 48, the rooms are decorated for Christmas. Presents are piled under a tree lit with candles. The halls are decked with holly and ivy. There are evergreens on the mantel of each fireplace. Wreaths and red bows are hung throughout the four-story building, and there is Christmas sheet music on the piano. It's all very merry, until a tall professor in a green sweater reads aloud: "Once upon a time—of all the good days in the year, on Christmas Eve—old Scrooge sat busy in his counting-house."

Meet Ebenezer Scrooge, one of beloved

British author Charles Dickens's most famous characters. Or as Dickens described him: "Scrooge! A squeezing, wrenching, grasping, scraping, clutching, covetous old sinner!" Scrooge is the main character in Dickens's short novel *A Christmas Carol.* That is what the professor is reading for his audience at 48 Doughty Street, the London town house that was once the home of Charles Dickens and his family that is now a museum.

Every Christmas, performances like this take place on the radio, at schools, in libraries, and in other public places. It is an annual holiday tradition for many people to buy tickets to see a play or a musical production of *A Christmas Carol.* Many more watch movie versions of Dickens's popular Christmas tale. There are even festivals dedicated to *A Christmas Carol.* People re-create Dickens's world. They dress up in clothes from the 1800s, sing carols, and serve food like sugarplums and fruitcake. Actors stroll around in costumes. They look and talk like the men, women, children—*and ghosts*—in the book. Everyone is on the lookout for Scrooge!

But what makes so many people want to gasp, boo, hiss, or clap for the main character of a book written nearly 180 years ago? Who *is* this Ebenezer Scrooge, and what exactly is his story?

CHAPTER 1
A Man of Many Words

Ebenezer Scrooge is a fictional character. But his last name is now a real word used for anyone who is mean, coldhearted, or cheap. This is thanks to the power of Charles Dickens's writing.

Charles Dickens

Dickens was born in Portsmouth, England, in 1812. He never finished school but still grew up to be one of  the world's most famous authors. The life he led was an education in itself.

Charles was one of eight children. His father, John Dickens, was not very good with money. He spent more of it than he earned. When Charles

was ten years old, the family moved to Camden Town, a neighborhood in London. Life there was difficult. The Dickens family lived in a series of cramped, often cold, homes. They were in debt because John Dickens owed money to so many people and shops.

Charles, who loved reading and learning, had to leave school at age twelve. He went to work in a factory. His job was to paste labels onto pots of blacking, a kind of shoe polish. The factory was dirty, smelly, and overrun with rats. Charles worked ten hours a day. Meanwhile, John Dickens, his wife, and most of their other children ended up in debtors' prison. They stayed there until John's debts were repaid. Charles was angry, sad, and embarrassed about his job and his family's situation. Later in life, he did not tell people about his stressful childhood. But he never forgot what it was like to be poor and miserable.

The Poor Get Poorer

Debtors' prisons were jails that held people who had borrowed money and still owed it. Often their loved ones were imprisoned, too, like Dickens's own family. During the 1800s, thousands of people in England were thrown into these jails. Some debtors' prisons housed criminals as well.

To get out of debtors' prison, inmates had to repay the money they owed. They were also charged fees for their stay in jail! Debtors who could pay for the privilege were allowed to work outside the jail during the day to earn money to pay their bills. Those who could not afford the prison or privilege fees got poorer and poorer the longer they remained in jail. Many of them starved and died there.

Other people who could not support themselves ended up in workhouses. They paid for their food and lodging there by working. Many inmates had jobs maintaining the workhouse and its kitchen. Other labor was difficult, boring work, such as breaking stones into the gravel used for roads or pulling apart old ropes for reuse in shipbuilding. Workhouse sleeping rooms were often crowded and cramped. But some young street children who ended up there did receive a basic education.

Dickens was a smart and energetic person. He was determined to be successful at something. At first, he wasn't sure what. When he was fifteen, Charles worked as a clerk in a law firm. Sometimes he entertained his bosses there. Dickens imitated

colorful Londoners he saw throughout the city. He acted out funny scenes of things that happened on the streets. He also taught himself shorthand, a quick way of taking notes. This helped him get jobs as a journalist when he was seventeen.

For several years, Dickens reported on government issues and court cases. In 1833, his first short story was published in a magazine. He also wrote articles about everyday people for various newspapers. These sketches were very popular. They led to Dickens being offered a job as a magazine editor. Charles worked hard as an editor. He became friends with other authors. He continued with his own writing as well. Dickens began producing novels. They were published as serials. That means one chapter of the novel was published in each issue of a magazine. Readers bought the magazine regularly. For authors, this meant a new chapter was due every month. Sometimes Charles wrote as many as ninety pages a month. And this was in addition to his editing work.

Charles Dickens lived and wrote during a period of great change called the Industrial Revolution. This revolution started in Great

Britain and dramatically changed how people lived and worked. It helped create the modern world.

Charles Dickens was an excellent storyteller. He was fascinated by city life and the variety of Londoners around him. Being a reporter had made him a sharp and accurate observer of people.

The Industrial Revolution

Until the late 1700s, most people lived in the countryside. They worked on farms or in small businesses. They made almost everything by hand. Then inventors found ways to harness steam and waterpower. This led to machines that could make many products—and make them fast! Factories were built. Different ways to process iron, steel, and coal were developed. Factory machines became even more productive. Railroad and steamship lines expanded. Trains and boats were needed to move

raw materials and manufactured goods from place to place. And people left the farms for paying jobs at these new businesses, which were located mainly in or near cities.

In 1800, less than 10 percent of the world's population lived in cities. One million people lived in London, England. Fifty years later, the population had more than doubled. London had become the biggest city in the world. What the Industrial Revolution meant for the rich, the working class, and the poor was an important theme in Dickens's work, especially in *A Christmas Carol*.

He had witnessed how the law, business, and the courts worked. He saw that the poor were not always treated justly. His personal life had made him sympathetic to how difficult and unfair life could be for many people. With pen, ink, wit, and wisdom, Charles Dickens brought all this to life on the page. By the time he was thirty, he had published five novels. Most of them were wildly popular. Even Queen Victoria, ruler of England at the time, read his books.

In 1843, Dickens introduced a new character to his devoted readers and a new word to the world: *Scrooge*!

Queen Victoria

CHAPTER 2
A Good Idea for a Book

Charles Dickens had a lot on his mind in 1843. He was still thrilled to be living in London. The city was exciting! Dickens especially loved going to the theater. He knew many interesting people. He enjoyed his growing fame as a writer. He had even traveled to the United States in 1842 on an author tour. But he could not ignore how so many British people were forced to live and work.

The Industrial Revolution changed everyone's lives. But that change wasn't equal. The rich got richer. They built mansions and bought art and other expensive things to fill them. Wealthy families lived well. Sometimes, they shared their wealth. They paid for the construction of libraries and museums. Or they set up charities to help people. A middle class of factory owners, merchants, and lawyers grew. They could afford to buy homes and educate their children, too.

But many jobs didn't pay well. Factory work was noisy and often unsafe. Workers lived in dirty, crowded shacks or rundown buildings. Unemployed people had it even worse. Whole families starved on city streets. Dickens was particularly shocked by a government report about the terrible lives of poor children. They worked in mines or factories for ten, twelve, or more hours a day. Their jobs were dangerous and paid little. Sometimes, small children had to actually climb into factory machines to fix them.

London Fog

The Industrial Revolution changed how Londoners worked and the city they worked in! Smoke billowed from chimneys, factories, chemical plants, and steamboats on the River Thames. The air was polluted.

London was also famous for its thick, soupy fogs. In the middle of one afternoon in the 1840s, factory smoke became trapped inside a dense fog. The city's polluted skies became pitch-black. Day turned into night! Londoners had to go about their business in the dark.

During the Industrial Revolution, some people profited from other people's misery. Dickens was angry about this. He said he wanted to "strike a sledgehammer blow" to help reform or change things.

Meanwhile, his responsibilities at home had increased. In 1836, Dickens married Catherine Hogarth. She was the daughter of a newspaper editor he knew. Within seven years, Charles and Catherine had four children—and a fifth child was on the way. His latest novel had not sold well. Dickens needed money. He turned to his sharpest tool: his words.

Catherine Hogarth

Dickens decided to write a Christmas book. He thought this would earn him some money.

But he also wanted his story to raise thoughtful questions: Why does society favor some people and not others? How are wealth and poverty connected? What should be done about suffering and injustice? Most important, he wanted his readers to think about what it truly means to be a good, loving human being.

To accomplish all this, Charles Dickens came up with the perfect villain: Ebenezer Scrooge! Then he set about writing his Christmas book.

It took Charles Dickens only six weeks to complete *A Christmas Carol*. The book is almost thirty thousand words long. And it's a most unusual holiday story. For one thing, its main character, Scrooge, *hates* Christmas. He is a disagreeable, unlikable businessman who cares only about himself and money. He ignores his only relative, his cheerful nephew, Fred. He is unkind to his sole employee, the hardworking clerk, Bob Cratchit. Bob's hours are long and his pay low. Stingy Scrooge won't even provide enough coal to keep the office warm! Still, at the end of each day, the clerk goes home to his poor but jolly and loving family. Scrooge heads back to the big, gloomy house where he lives alone.

Clearly, Dickens is setting up a story in which Ebenezer Scrooge needs to learn some important life lessons. The surprising thing about this holiday tale is who will teach him those lessons: ghosts!

A Fine Edition

Because selling Christmas books was a new idea in Dickens's time, he wanted to make sure his holiday book was beautiful and affordable.

A Christmas Carol was published on December 19, 1843. The book had a red cloth cover with gold lettering on the front and spine. The edges of its pages were gold, too. Artist John Leech provided the illustrations, some in color. It was Leech who gave Ebenezer Scrooge his now-famous look as a tall, thin man with a long pointy nose and a deep frown.

The original six thousand printed copies sold out within days. *A Christmas Carol* has never since been out of print.

CHAPTER 3
Bah! Humbug!

"Marley was dead to begin with." That's a strange way to begin a Christmas story! The unnamed narrator of *A Christmas Carol* explains that Jacob Marley was Ebenezer Scrooge's business partner. But now "Old Marley was as dead as a doornail." Then the narrator introduces Scrooge.

Here is a man whose "cold within him froze his old features, nipped his pointed nose, shriveled his cheek, stiffened his gait [his way of walking], made his eyes red, his thin lips blue . . ."

Scrooge walks to and from work, ignoring the weather, everyone he passes, and even tail-wagging dogs. No one dares to say hello to him. He's never stopped and asked for directions or the time. Beggars shrink from him and never ask him for money. Scrooge is fine with all this. He likes to keep people at a distance.

Scrooge owns a counting-house. His company
lends money and keeps track of business accounts
and finances. At the beginning of *A Christmas
Carol*, Scrooge is working at his counting-house
on Christmas Eve. So is his clerk, Bob Cratchit,

who spends long hours at his desk in a cold corner of the office. He has to huddle around a candle to keep warm! Although Ebenezer himself started as a clerk in a warehouse, he does not pay his own clerk very much. Cratchit can barely support his wife and six children. He cannot afford care for his sickly son, Tiny Tim. He doesn't even own a winter coat! Still, Bob Cratchit looks forward to spending Christmas day with his family.

Bob Cratchit and Tiny Tim

A Clerk's Job

Charles Dickens had worked as a clerk. He knew all about the job he gave Bob Cratchit.

The Industrial Revolution expanded business and trade in London. This meant there were more business deals, accounting records, official documents, legal papers, bills, receipts, and various other files and records that had to be written by hand. Any copies had to be handwritten as well. Clerks spent hours at their desks, sitting on hard wooden stools and scribbling away. They also had to deliver messages and collect payments. They even had to stoke the office coal fire—unless they worked for someone as cheap as Scrooge!

Ebenezer Scrooge does not care about the
holiday. His nephew, Fred, drops by to invite
him for Christmas dinner. Scrooge refuses to
go. "Every idiot who goes about with 'Merry
Christmas' on his lips should be boiled with his
own pudding . . . ," he snaps. When Fred wishes

him a "merry Christmas," his cranky uncle replies, "Bah! Humbug!" That became Scrooge's most famous line! But what exactly *is* a *humbug*?

Two well-fed, well-dressed businessmen visit Scrooge in his office. In the spirit of Christmas, they are collecting money to "buy the Poor some meat and drink and means of warmth." Scrooge smugly suggests that the poor can go to debtors' prison or the workhouse instead. He is

What's a Humbug?

Humbug is something that is false, dishonest, or a trick of sorts. The word came into use in the 1750s. No one knows for sure from where. An eighteenth-century dictionary defined the word *hum* as "to deceive." An early twentieth-century encyclopedia suggests a connection with Hamburg, Germany. At one time, fake coins were produced there. So maybe *Hamburg* became *humbug* to mean "fake."

But Scrooge's use of the word is clear. He means holidays are a silly fraud, celebrating is a waste of time, and even Christmas is *humbug*!

not concerned about the conditions in either of those places. He feels that if the poor die there, it's not much of a loss. That means fewer people to support. Scrooge sends the businessmen away without a penny.

When a young boy sings a Christmas carol outside the office door, Scrooge chases him off with a ruler. Finally, by nightfall, it's time to

close the office. Scrooge growls at Bob Cratchit for taking off the next day, Christmas. Then the cranky old man heads home alone.

The cruel things Scrooge says and does on Christmas Eve will come back to haunt him . . . *that very night*!

The way to Scrooge's home is dark and dreary. As he puts his key in the front-door lock, a strange light hovers over it. And then the door knocker transforms into a face! For an instant, Jacob Marley stares straight at Scrooge.

A startled Scrooge scurries inside and checks all round his dim, gloomy house. "Humbug," he decides and changes into his bedclothes. He sits in front of a barely flickering fire and sips thin soup.

Suddenly, all the bells in the house start ringing! There's a deep, clanging boom in the cellar. Something is noisily dragged up the stairs.

The clanging grows louder and closer. And then there, standing right in front of Scrooge, is Jacob Marley. The ghost is covered in thick iron chains. Metal locks, keys, cash boxes, and other tools of the counting business hang heavy all over him. And yet the ghost passed through the thick, bolted, double-locked door. Ebenezer can look right through his long-dead partner's body. And he still doesn't believe what he sees!

Scrooge insists that an upset stomach is making him imagine things. He thinks that he must have eaten something bad. He tells Marley's ghost, "You may be an undigested bit of beef . . . an underdone potato. There's more of gravy than of grave about you, whatever you are!"

But Marley knows better. The dead man is doomed to wander as a ghost in chains because in life he was a greedy, uncaring person. Just like his partner. Marley has come to offer Scrooge a very special Christmas gift. "I am here tonight to warn

you," he says, "that you have yet a chance and hope of escaping my fate."

Scrooge is shocked to hear who will deliver this hopeful gift . . .

"You will be haunted by Three Spirits," Marley tells Scrooge.

CHAPTER 4
Rise!

Marley's ghost—chains and all—floats out the window. It joins other unhappy souls wandering around and moaning in the night sky. These ghosts are also weighed down with chains and heavy metal objects. They, too, want to make up for being mean and selfish people when they were alive. But it is too late. The living can't see them.

Ebenezer Scrooge tries to say "Humbug!" once again in response to the whole evening's events. But this time, he just can't get the word out. He falls asleep. When he awakes, he wonders if he'd been dreaming. *Or . . .*

The clock strikes one. The curtains around Scrooge's bed are slowly drawn open. A bright light flashes.

The first ghost! Just as Marley predicted.

Scrooge huddles in bed and stares at the "unearthly visitor." The bright light is shooting out from the crown of its head. The ghost is small, like a child. But it also has strong arms and legs, and long white hair like an old man. The spirit carries a cap and wears a short belted robe. The belt sparkles off and on, which makes the ghost seem to change shape. Its head disappears. Twenty legs appear. Scrooge is confused: What *is* it?

"I am the Ghost of Christmas Past . . . Your past."

The spirit commands: "Rise! And walk with me!" They pass right through the wall of Scrooge's house. London disappears behind them, and Ebenezer and the ghost stand in a country road, surrounded by snow-covered fields. It is where Scrooge grew up.

Scrooge recognizes everything and everyone along the road they walk. Cries of "Merry Christmas!" ring out. People are headed home for the holiday. The ghost and Scrooge keep going. They enter a large, depressing brick building. The windows are cracked and the walls are damp. In a bare, unwelcoming schoolroom, they spy a little boy reading a book. Scrooge begins to cry.

It is his own young, pitiful self, left behind at Christmas!

Scrooge remembers being that lonely boy. He used to imagine that characters from books kept him company. He happily recalls being surrounded by Ali Baba; Aladdin with his genie; and Robinson Crusoe  with his talking green parrot. And then Ebenezer grows sad. He remembers another poor boy, the one who sang a carol outside his office door. "I should like to have given him something," Scrooge tells the ghost. But the spirit has already led them forward in time.

Once again, it's Christmas at the bleak school. Young Ebenezer is a little older but still alone, still sad. That changes the minute the school door opens. There's his sister, Fan! Their strict father has changed his ways. Ebenezer is

now welcome at home. She is going to take him
there for Christmas. Old Scrooge dearly loved
Fan.

The ghost reminds him that Fan left behind a child when she died. Scrooge squirms. He's thinking of his earlier, rude conversation with Fan's son, his nephew, Fred.

The Ghost of Christmas Past moves on. Scrooge and this first spirit have returned to the city. Ebenezer now sees himself at work as a young clerk in a warehouse. His boss, Mr. Fezziwig, has just declared, "Yo ho, my boys! No more work tonight. Christmas Eve . . ." The warehouse is set up as a ballroom. Mr. Fezziwig and his wife host a lively Christmas party for their workers and neighbors. The fire is blazing. The table is filled with cakes, pies, meats, and drinks. A fiddler is playing merrily and everyone is dancing. As he and the ghost watch, Scrooge's "heart and soul were in the scene with his former self." The ghost notes that Fezziwig had to spend only a little money on such a good time for all.

Scrooge replies, "The happiness he gives is quite as great as if it cost a fortune." Then the old miser (someone who hoards money and spends little) thinks about how poorly he treated his own clerk, Bob Cratchit.

Scrooge's strange journey with this ghost isn't finished yet. The small spirit whisks him away to another time and place. Now Ebenezer is a grown man with a "greedy, restless motion" about him.

Scrooge and Belle

He is with a beautiful young woman named Belle. They were once in love. But Scrooge has found a stronger passion: money. Sadly, Belle breaks their engagement. The scene changes again.

Belle is shown happily married, surrounded by her laughing, playful children. They are all excited about Christmas. Old Scrooge envies her. To make it worse, Belle's husband comes home and says he just saw "Mr. Scrooge. . . . Quite alone in the world, I do believe."

Ebenezer can't take any more of this visit. "Haunt me no longer!" he cries. He seizes the ghost's cap and pulls it down over the spirit's head to extinguish its light. Then Scrooge falls back into bed, asleep.

In writing this chapter, Charles Dickens may have remembered his own lonely feelings as a child, separated from his family. Dickens makes the point that too much love of money leaves too little room for loving others. Greed can certainly change a person for the worse.

But it will take more than one ghost to get Ebenezer Scrooge to fully see this, too.

CHAPTER 5
The Bell Sounds Again

When the bell sounds again, Scrooge is ready. He creeps toward a ghostly light in his other room. Inside, the logs in the fireplace blaze. The walls and ceiling are covered in mistletoe, berries, holly, and ivy.

"Come in! . . . and know me better, man!" a giant in a dark green robe calls out to Scrooge. He has long hair crowned with a wreath of holly and icicles. He holds a glowing torch and sits on a throne made of food: cooked meats, piles of roasted poultry, chains of sausages, mouthwatering pies, and juicy apples, oranges, and pears.

"I am the Ghost of Christmas Present."

This giant spirit is joyful and kind-looking.

Scrooge humbly asks if the ghost has anything
to teach him. At the giant's command, the old
man grabs hold of the spirit's green robe, and
they are off.

The Ghost of Christmas Present and Ebenezer Scrooge stroll through London's bustling streets unseen. Everyone is preparing for Christmas. Sidewalks are shoveled free of snow. Grocers sell the last of their holiday treats. Shoppers juggle overflowing baskets through groups of children throwing snowballs. The delicious scents of warm chestnuts, tangy fruit, and sweet candies waft everywhere. Some people dressed in their finest clothes head to church. Others head to bakeries. They carry their dinners through the streets. The poor don't have ovens at home. Bakers cook meager Christmas meals for them in their shops. The Ghost of Christmas Present blesses all this food with a sprinkling of his torch. Scrooge watches as he does the same when they reach the doorway of a small house. They have reached the Cratchit home.

The Cratchits are clearly a poor family. Their house is a tiny space for eight people. It's clear

Mrs. Cratchit's dress has been mended several times. Bob Cratchit's clothes are shabby but clean. Oldest daughter Martha works long hours as a hatmaker. The youngest boy, Tiny Tim, is cheerful as he hobbles over to his stool by the fire in their cramped home. But he is small and weak.

Three of the other Cratchit children parade

in with the cooked goose for Christmas dinner, back from the baker's oven. Everyone at the table cheers. Applesauce and mashed potatoes are passed around. When Mrs. Cratchit's special Christmas pudding is served for dessert, it's declared "wonderful." No one mentions it's a small portion for such a large family.

Real-Life Characters

Charles Dickens created some of the most unforgettable characters in fiction. A few of them were inspired by real people.

Both Charles Dickens and Ebenezer Scrooge had a beloved sister named Fanny. Frederick Dickens was Charles's favorite brother. The author named Scrooge's cheerful nephew Fred.

Tiny Tim

Tiny Tim is the son of Scrooge's clerk, Bob Cratchit. The boy's health is poor. He wears a leg brace and walks with a crutch. Tiny Tim was inspired by a member of the author's own family: Dickens's nephew Henry Burnett was disabled and died when he was only nine.

After dinner, the Cratchits snuggle around the fire. Bob proposes a toast. They'll have to share the drinks, though. The Cratchits own only two glasses and a small cup with no handle. "A Merry Christmas to us all, my dears," Mr. Cratchit says. "God bless us every one!" replies Tiny Tim. This simple sentence becomes one of the most famous lines in a Dickens book. Even Ebenezer Scrooge, secretly watching, is moved by the little boy's good heart!

Scrooge asks the Ghost of Christmas Present whether Tiny Tim will live.

The giant replies that if nothing changes, the boy will die. Scrooge begs, "Oh, no, kind Spirit! Say he will be spared." The ghost mocks Ebenezer with his own words about letting the poor die to decrease the population. Scrooge is sorry and ashamed. He grows more so when kindly Bob Cratchit includes his employer in a toast. The Cratchit family reluctantly joins in. Scrooge can see that "the mention of his name cast a dark shadow on the party, which was not dispelled for full five minutes."

But the Cratchits are a loving family, all grateful for one another. Their holiday merrymaking starts up again as Scrooge is carried away by the ghost. The miserable old man can't help glancing back at Tiny Tim.

Night is coming, and snow is falling heavily now on the London streets. People rush toward their well-lit homes filled with family and friends. They are eager to celebrate the holiday together. The Ghost of Christmas Present is delighted to see this. He sprinkles happiness on them all.

And then the city disappears. Scrooge and the spirit are in a bleak, gloomy, rocky land. They reach a mud-and-stone hut. Several generations of a family are huddled inside. But the family members are wearing festive clothes. The oldest among them loudly sings a holiday song. "Miners . . . who labor in the bowels of the earth," explains

the Ghost of Christmas Present. "But they know me." The giant and Scrooge speed over other far-flung places where people know and celebrate the spirit of Christmas, too. In a lonely lighthouse tower, the two keepers shake hands and wish each other a Merry Christmas. On a ship way out at sea, sailors hum Christmas tunes.

Suddenly, the howling sound of wind and waves turns into a hearty "Ha, ha, ha!" Thanks to the giant ghost, Scrooge has ended up at his nephew's Christmas dinner after all. And he is the main topic!

Fred's wife and dinner guests talk about what a cranky, mean-spirited old man Scrooge is. But Fred insists he will still continue to invite his uncle for Christmas. "I mean to give him the same

chance every year, whether he likes it or not," he says, "for I pity him."

Ebenezer finds himself deeply moved by the music Fred's wife plays on her harp. It makes him seriously consider what he's slowly learning about kindness from the two ghosts' visits. Then before he can stop himself, Scrooge is playing along in their party games, even though they can't hear the answers he shouts out. Everyone joins Fred as he toasts "Uncle Scrooge." Scrooge himself feels so very "light of heart" that he'd like to toast Fred back. But the spirit has other plans.

Scrooge holds on to the ghost's robe as they travel from jail cells to hospital rooms to

poorhouses. The Ghost of Christmas Present blesses and comforts everyone. No one Scrooge has seen this night is as wealthy as he. Yet all of them who had so much less still celebrated so much more.

At last, Scrooge and the giant ghost stand together alone. Scrooge notices something strange poking out from under the green hem of the giant's robe. The Ghost of Christmas Present opens his wrap. At his feet are two ragged, angry, frightening children. "This boy is Ignorance. This girl is Want," says the ghost sadly. They look like many of the poor children in London at the time.

Scrooge is horrified and asks if there is no help or home for them. "Are there no prisons? Are there no workhouses?" the spirit replies. The very answer Scrooge himself gave earlier when asked for a donation for the poor.

Rough and Ragged Childhoods

Charles Dickens worked hard as a child. Still, he was better off than many other children at the time. In the 1830s, nearly half the funerals held in London were for children under ten. By 1850, fifteen to twenty thousand poor, homeless people were living—and dying—on the city's streets.

Volunteers created "Ragged Schools" in poor neighborhoods. They fed and taught homeless and starving children. Dickens visited a "Ragged School" in 1843. Most students had only rags or torn clothes to wear, which is where the name came from. The

 visit was an inspiration for *A Christmas Carol* and for its heartbreaking characters, including the poor children he named Ignorance and Want.

Now even Scrooge cannot deny what the Ghosts of Christmas Past and Christmas Present have shown him. His selfishness affects so many other people. He has been thoughtless about those who work for him and careless about those who love him. He is merciless to the poor and blames them for their poverty. Scrooge has lived in his own world with only one inhabitant, himself.

He wonders—*and dreads*—what may come next!

CHAPTER 6
Merry Christmas!

The third and final ghost is unlike the other two. Its face and body are hidden by a long, hooded robe. The robe is so dark, it blends into the night. All Ebenezer can see is an outstretched hand. This ghost floats toward him "like a mist along the ground."

Scrooge knows he's been shown the past and present. He immediately realizes who this spirit is. "Ghost of the Future! I fear you more . . .

But I know your purpose is to do me good . . . ,"
he cries. The spirit doesn't answer. He just carries
Scrooge away in his shadow.

Walking Through Scrooge's World

Ebenezer Scrooge and the three Christmas ghosts travel through a noisy and crowded world. Charles Dickens's colorful descriptions make this world come alive.

All his life, Dickens enjoyed going on very long walks. He particularly liked strolling around London at night, when most other people were asleep. He roamed through fashionable neighborhoods

and shabby slums. He knew all the streets, alleys, and lanes of the big city. Walking was a good way for the author to collect details about different people and places. That information inspired his writing.

Dickens said he composed *A Christmas Carol* in his head while walking. Some of those walks were fifteen to twenty miles long! He would often be laughing and crying as he strode along thinking of the plot for his book. Ebenezer Scrooge was created on the same streets in which his story takes place!

The silent spirit and the trembling man are in the business hall where Scrooge used to gather with colleagues. He does not seem himself standing in his usual place. He overhears the other businessmen laughing about someone who has died. They joke that they'll go to the funeral only if lunch is served after. Scrooge has no idea who they are talking about.

From there, the two of them move down a filthy, narrow alley. Scrooge and the ghost enter a grimy little shop. It's filled with greasy rags, battered junk, and even old bones. A pipe-smoking old man sits in the middle of all the clutter. He buys and sells these scraps. Three people enter: a cleaning woman, a laundry woman, and an undertaker. They all have goods to sell to the shopkeeper—all stolen from the same house where a man has just died alone. The cleaning woman laughs and says, "He frightened every one away from him when he was alive, to profit us when he was dead!" She means the dead man had no family or friends, so his servants were free to take his belongings and sell them. Scrooge wonders who this man could have been.

The Ghost of Christmas Future takes Scrooge through the city streets to a dark, scary room. Just as the cleaning woman had said, it has been robbed of everything—even the blankets and the shirt the dead man was dressed in for burial. A corpse lies on the bed, alone. The ghost points, but Scrooge is afraid to go see who the dead man is. He begs the spirit to show him anyone "who feels emotion caused by this man's death."

The spirit reveals a young couple. But they are not sad. They are thankful the man is dead. He would have ruined them because of a debt they owed to him. Their glad relief is the only emotion anyone feels about the dead man.

Scrooge grows uneasy. He asks the spirit to show him "some tenderness connected with a death." To his horror, the Ghost of Christmas Future takes him through London to the Cratchits' house. It is decorated for Christmas but very quiet. No one is celebrating. Mrs. Cratchit is sewing, but it seems like she's been crying. The younger children are "as still as statues."

The stool in the corner near the fireplace is empty. Tiny Tim has died. Bob Cratchit returns from arranging the funeral. He goes upstairs to the bed where the little body of his son lies, awaiting burial. He kisses Tiny Tim goodbye and then comes back down. Bob tells his family he met Scrooge's nephew, Fred, in the street. Fred has been kind and offered them any help they may need. The Cratchits comfort one another and vow never to forget sweet little Tiny Tim.

Scrooge is really worried now. He dares to ask the name of the dead man they saw. The hooded ghost leads him to a churchyard cemetery. It is weedy and overgrown. The spooky hand points down at a neglected gravestone. Scrooge won't look. He asks if everything the Ghost of Christmas Future has shown him *will* happen or only *may* happen. Silently, the spirit points again. The terrified man creeps closer to the grave. The tombstone reads: EBENEZER SCROOGE.

Scrooge grabs the spirit's long, dark robe. He swears: "I am not the man I was!" Then Ebenezer asks one of the most important questions of the book: "Why show me this, if I am past all hope?"

The ghost seems shaken that Ebenezer is asking for another chance. Because of what the three ghosts have shown him, Scrooge wants to rethink the way he lives before it is too late. As he prays for this, the Ghost of Christmas Future shrinks away.

Ebenezer Scrooge wakes up in his own bed. He's overjoyed to wake up at all!

Thanks to the three ghosts, he is a changed man. "I will live in the Past, the Present, and the Future!" Scrooge declares as he jumps out of bed. He is positively giddy. He does something he never did before. He laughs out loud! He is "as happy as an angel." And then he prepares to celebrate Christmas. But this time, he'll do things the right way—by helping others.

Scrooge immediately hires a boy in the street to take the Cratchits a turkey "twice the size of Tiny Tim." He finds one of the businessmen collecting for the poor and surprises him with a big donation. He walks the streets of London wishing everyone "Merry Christmas!"

Then he arrives at Fred's Christmas party. Scrooge is nervous and humble, but Fred and his wife welcome him. Uncle Scrooge feels "at home in five minutes." He enthusiastically joins in the dinner and games. He declares the whole evening a "wonderful party . . . won-der-ful happiness!"

The day after Christmas, Ebenezer Scrooge sticks to his new plan to do good. He playfully scolds Bob Cratchit for arriving late at the office. Then he shocks his clerk by clapping him on the back, wishing him well, and giving him a big raise. And he promises to help the struggling Cratchit family.

Scrooge keeps his word on this. He becomes almost a second father to Tiny Tim. The miser who was once such a loner now shares his wealth and makes friends all around the city. Scrooge, who was once hated, is now hailed as a good man. And if anyone thought otherwise, Ebenezer's "own heart laughed: and that was quite enough for him."

CHAPTER 7
The Father of Christmas

Ebenezer Scrooge is changed forever by one long, unforgettable night. For the rest of his life, he's known as a man who "knew how to keep Christmas well."

Through telling Scrooge's story, Charles Dickens became known as "the Father of Christmas."

A Christmas Carol was very popular. Scenes from the book showed many jolly holiday celebrations from the time, like Londoners decorating their homes and shops, preparing special feasts, singing, dancing, and having a good time. Dickens's novel helped bring back Christmas traditions like caroling. The book also promoted new customs, such as Christmas trees, which were then just becoming popular in England. Decorated Christmas trees had been introduced to Great Britain in the mid-nineteenth century by Prince Albert, the German-born husband of Queen Victoria.

Ebenezer Scrooge changed from a "Bah! Humbug" man to someone who wished everyone "Merry Christmas." The greeting became more commonly used because of Dickens's book. Printed Christmas cards also first appeared in 1843, the year *A Christmas Carol* was published.

Charles Dickens became closely linked to Christmas. He wrote *A Christmas Carol* in protest of the gap between rich and poor people. But his unusual book also helped establish Christmas as a major holiday celebration in nineteenth-century England. It has remained so.

Happy Holiday

Billions of Christians around the world celebrate Christmas on December 25 each year. They honor the birth of Jesus Christ.

But the day was not always festive. For example, the Pilgrims who came to America in 1620 did not believe in holiday merrymaking. They even banned Christmas celebrations in their Massachusetts Bay Colony!

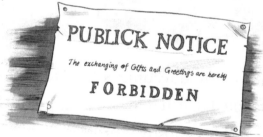

Christmas became an official holiday in England in 1834, the year *A Christmas Carol* was published. It became a federal holiday in the United States on June 26, 1870.

People enjoyed reading *A Christmas Carol*. But they also liked to listen to it. The story of Ebenezer Scrooge and his ghostly visitors thrilled audiences that came to hear Charles Dickens himself read it aloud. *A Christmas Carol* was Dickens's first public reading. The performance took place in Birmingham, England, on December 27, 1853.

As a young man, Dickens had gone to the theater in London almost every night. His love of plays and other shows helped him become an excellent reader of his own books. He practiced different expressions for his characters in a mirror. He made notes, or prompts, in a copy of a book to improve his performance while reading it aloud.

Charles Dickens was really good at imitating people. He used different voices for a book's characters. He was spooky and mysterious when the ghosts appear in *A Christmas Carol*. He was cranky, confused, terrified, and joyful as Ebenezer Scrooge. Dickens was a lively and dramatic

performer. For the audience, it felt like all the people from *A Christmas Carol* were right onstage with him!

Americans loved his performances, too. They flocked to hear Dickens read when he toured the United States during 1867–1868. *A Christmas Carol* was the work he performed most often. The author gave seventy-six readings in eighteen cities. The events sold out. People camped overnight to buy passes. President Andrew Jackson bought tickets for his family for every night that Dickens performed in Washington, DC. Audiences sobbed over the famous last line of the book, a repeat of Tiny Tim's toast: "God bless Us, Every One!"

In Boston, Massachusetts, a wealthy businessman heard Dickens read. He was so moved by *A Christmas Carol* that he closed his factory on Christmas and gave his workers the day off. Then he sent all of them each a turkey, just like Scrooge did for the Cratchits.

A Christmas Carol promoted charitable giving. Holiday spending came to mean donating to the less fortunate, too. More people remembered that the spirit of Christmas was generosity. And that was just the kind of impact Dickens hoped his book would have.

CHAPTER 8
Scrooge Lives On

The story of Ebenezer Scrooge is all about hope and redemption (being saved from sin or evil). It is the story of a man who is moved to leave his greedy and solitary life behind so he can create a more generous and fulfilling one. These are central ideas that Dickens wanted to share with readers of *A Christmas Carol*. They are also part of the spiritual meaning of Christmas itself.

Scrooge's redemption story in *A Christmas Carol* inspired many readers. They gave to charity. They opened their eyes to how other people lived, especially children. They began to demand changes from business and political leaders. This was all very important to Dickens. It was a big part of the reason he wrote *A Christmas Carol*.

Dickens was concerned with how society treated those without money or power. He believed in reform, or changes, in laws and in housing, education, and employment opportunities that would improve the lives of workers and the poor. And he believed that people in real life who were well-off like Ebenezer Scrooge had a responsibility to make those changes happen.

Dickens wrote *A Christmas Carol,* along with many other books and articles, to encourage the good works and improvements he wanted to see happen in his world. In 1850, he also started a weekly magazine, *Household Words.* Much of it— both fiction and nonfiction—dealt with social, economic, and political issues. And because *A Christmas Carol* was such a success, Dickens wrote and published other Christmas stories in his magazine every holiday.

Scrooge's story was Charles Dickens's last public reading. By then, he was fifty-eight years old and in ill health. Still, on March 15, 1870, thousands crowded into Saint James Hall in London to hear the author read from *A Christmas Carol*. When he was finished, Dickens bowed and said: "From these garish lights I vanish now forevermore, with a heartfelt, grateful, respectful, and affectionate farewell."

Three months later, he was dead.

Over the course of his life, Charles Dickens wrote fifteen novels and dozens of short stories. None of his novels, including *A Christmas Carol*, has ever gone out of print. For thirty-four years, between 1836 and 1870, readers could buy magazines with new writing by Dickens! But when the holidays came in December each year, many people turned again to his classic, *A Christmas Carol*.

Twenty-first-century audiences, like those that gathered to watch Dickens's tale in the nineteenth century, see the true, positive meaning of his Christmas ghost story. In a short note at the beginning of *A Christmas Carol*, Dickens wrote: "I have endeavoured [tried] in this Ghostly little book, to raise the Ghost of an Idea, which shall not put my readers out of humour with themselves, with each other, with the season, or with me."

Scrooge Goes to the Movies

Dickens's famous Christmas story inspired various holiday movies—more than 150 of them!

In the late 1850s, important scenes from the book were painted on glass slides. The colorful slides were then projected and enlarged through a magic lantern, a type of early projector. In the 1901 silent film *Scrooge; or, Marley's Ghost*, the spirit looks silly rather than spooky. The actor walks through the scenes clutching a sheet around his head! In this movie, Scrooge had to learn his lessons quickly—the entire movie was only six minutes and twenty seconds long!

The classic movie version of Dickens's story is the 1951 British film *Scrooge* (released as *A Christmas Carol* in the United States), starring Alastair Sim. It was supposed to open at Radio City Music Hall in New York City, but managers there thought it was too grim for their famous annual Christmas show. This black-and-white movie reached even wider audiences when television stations began broadcasting it every Christmas season.

Scrooge has been played by many famous faces. Patrick Stewart and Michael Caine have played Dickens's cranky old miser. Jim Carrey was the voice of Scrooge *and* all the ghosts in Disney's

2009 animated version of *A Christmas Carol*.

But stars don't have to be human to be Scrooge. There are movie versions of *A Christmas Carol* that feature Muppets, the Smurfs, Mickey Mouse and his cartoon friends, and even Barbie!

Dickens's "Ghost of an Idea"—that people should always try to be good and to *do* good—is timeless. It's an idea that Ebenezer Scrooge finally comes to understand. For as he vows at the end of his long, scary night with the spirits: "I yet may change these shadows you have shown me, by an altered life!" . . . "I will honour Christmas in my

heart, and try to keep it all the year." Scrooge,
the changed man, has become a role model for
everyone!

Bibliography

*Books for young readers

Ackroyd, Peter. *Dickens' London: An Imaginative Vision.*
London: Headline, 1987.

*Dickens, Charles. *A Christmas Carol.* New York, NY: Puffin
Classics, 2015.

Fido, Martin. *The World of Charles Dickens: The Life, Times and
Works of the Great Victorian Novelist.* London: Carlton
Books Limited, 2012.

Henson, Brian, director. *The Muppet Christmas Carol.* 1992;
Burbank, CA: Walt Disney Home Entertainment, 2005. DVD.

Hurst, Brian Desmond, director. *A Christmas Carol.* 1951; Tulsa, OK:
VCI Entertainment, 2007. DVD.

Jones, David Hugh, director. *A Christmas Carol.* 1999; Burbank, CA:
Warner Home Video, 2010. DVD.

Mattinson, Burny, director. *Mickey's Christmas Carol.* 1983;
Burbank, CA: Walt Disney Home Entertainment, 2013. DVD.

*McAllister, Angela. *A World Full of Dickens Stories : 8 Best-Loved Classic Tales Retold for Children*. Minneapolis: Frances Lincoln Children's Books/The Quarto Group, 2020.

*Pollack, Pam, and Meg Belviso. *Who Was Charles Dickens?* New York: Penguin Workshop, 2014.

*Rosen, Michael. *Dickens: His Work and His World*. Cambridge, MA: Candlewick Press, 2005.

Tomalin, Claire. *Charles Dickens: A Life*. New York: The Penguin Press, 2011.

Zemeckis, Robert, director. *Disney's A Christmas Carol*. 2009; Burbank, CA: Walt Disney Home Entertainment, 2010. DVD.

Websites

www.dickensfellowship.org

www.dickensmuseum.com

YOUR HEADQUARTERS FOR HISTORY

Activities, Mad Libs, and sidesplitting jokes!
Discover the Who HQ books beyond the biographies